EARTH

by L. L. Owens

The Child's World®

Published by The Child's World®
1980 Lookout Drive • Mankato, MN 56003-1705
800-599-READ • www.childsworld.com

ACKNOWLEDGMENTS
The Child's World®: Mary Berendes, Publishing Director
The Design Lab: Design and production
Red Line Editorial: Editorial direction

PHOTO CREDITS
NASA, cover, 1, 32; NASA/courtesy of nasaimages.org. cover, 1, 3, 4,
6, 10, 12, 14, 15, 18, 19, 23, 26, 29, 31; NASA/NSSDC/Catalog of
Spaceborne Imaging, 5; NASA/courtesy of nasaimages.org/The Design Lab,
6, 7; Don Nichols/iStockphoto, 9; NASA/The Design Lab, 11; Rob Friedman/
iStockphoto, 13; EpicStock/Shutterstock Images, 17; NASA/JPL/UCSD/JSC/
courtesy of nasaimages.org, 21; Rolf Fischer/iStockphoto, 25; Andrzej Stajer/
iStockphoto, 27

LIBRARY OF CONGRESS CATALOGING-IN-PUBLICATION DATA
Owens, L. L.
  Earth / by L. L. Owens.
      p. cm.
  Includes bibliographical references and index.
  ISBN 978-1-60954-381-5 (library bound : alk. paper)
  1. Earth—Juvenile literature. I. Title.
  QB631.4.O94 2011
  525—dc22
                              2010039957

Printed in the United States of America
Mankato, MN
December, 2010
PA02072

ON THE COVER

This image shows Earth's true colors. It was taken by the National Aeronautics and Space Administration (NASA), a US agency that studies space and the planets.

Table of Contents

Earth and the Solar System

Try holding up a big blue marble against a starry night sky. That is like what **astronauts** see when looking at Earth from space!

Earth is a planet in our **solar system**. Earth's space neighbors include seven other planets. At the center of our solar system is the sun. Planets go around, or **orbit**, the sun.

Fun Fact

Thousands of years ago, people noticed bright objects moving in the night sky. The word *planet* comes from the Greek word for "wanderer."

Earth's land areas are visible from space.

SUN

Mercury

Venus

Earth

Mars

Ceres

Jupiter

Fun Facts

PLANET NUMBER: Earth is the third planet from the sun.

DISTANCE FROM SUN: 93 million miles (150 million km)

SIZE: The distance around Earth's middle is about 24,900 miles (40,000 km). That is about as long as 365,000 football fields put together!

OUR SOLAR SYSTEM: Our solar system has eight planets and five **dwarf planets**. Pluto used to be called a planet. But in 2006, scientists decided to call it a dwarf planet instead. Scientists hope to discover even more dwarf planets in our solar system!

Saturn

Uranus

Neptune

Pluto

Haumea

Makemake

Eris

Planet

Dwarf Planet

The word *earth* is another name for ground. When the planet was named, people did not fly in planes or travel to space. The ground was their home. So it made sense to name the planet after it.

Soil and dirt are also called *earth*.

Earth's orbit around the sun takes about 365 days. That is one full year—or the time between your birthdays!

While orbiting the sun, a planet spins like a top. Imagine a line running through a planet from top to bottom. That's the planet's **axis**. Each planet spins, or rotates, on its axis. One rotation equals one day. Think of one day on a planet as the time from one sunrise to the next sunrise. An Earth day is 24 hours long.

Fun Fact

Earth's axis is not straight up and down. It is tilted at about 23 degrees. This tilt gives Earth its seasons.

An axis runs through the center of a planet. The planet spins on the axis.

An Invisible Force

Try tossing a ball into the air. What happens? It falls to the ground! **Gravity** is the force that pulls objects together. It's what draws all objects—including you—toward the ground. Strong gravity is what pulls Earth along its path orbiting the sun.

Fun Fact

As it orbits the sun, Earth spins on its axis at about 1,000 miles per hour (1,600 km/h). That's more than 15 times the average speed limit on a US highway! Gravity is what keeps you from flying off into space as the planet spins.

Earth's gravity is a strong force that pulls objects toward the planet. That's why this ball will come back down to Earth!

Earth's Moon

Gravity also keeps Earth's moon close. Scientists think that long ago, a large object hit Earth. It broke off huge chunks of the planet. Those pieces formed the moon. The moon has orbited Earth ever since.

Asteroids and other objects slammed into the moon, denting its surface. The moon's rocky surface is filled with deep **craters**.

Fun Fact

US astronauts first walked on the moon in 1969. They wore special space suits to help them breathe.

Craters dot the moon's
dusty surface.

Life on Earth

From space, Earth looks very blue. Water covers almost three-fourths of Earth's surface. So astronauts nicknamed Earth the Blue Planet.

This water is one reason why Earth is so special. As far as we know, life cannot survive without water. And Earth is the only planet we know with life on it.

Strong waves crash in Earth's oceans.

But water is not the only thing that makes Earth perfect for life. Earth is just the right distance from the scorching sun at the center of our solar system. If Earth were closer to the sun, the planet might be too hot for life to survive. The sun's heat would boil away the water. But if Earth were farther from the sun, we might freeze.

Fun Fact

Earth's hottest temperature was 136°F (58°C) in Libya, Africa, in 1922. The coldest temperature was –129°F (–89°C) in Antarctica in 1983.

Astronauts who traveled near the moon took this picture of Earth. From the far side of the moon, Earth appeared to rise above the moon's surface.

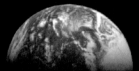

Earth's **atmosphere** also helps control the temperature. It traps heat from the sun, so we don't get too cold. At the same time, the atmosphere protects us from getting too hot. It is also the air that we breathe.

Earth's atmosphere is made of layers of **gas** that surround the planet like a blanket.

Earth's size gives its gravitational pull the right strength. A big object has a strong gravitational pull, and a small object has a weaker pull.

Remember what happens when you throw a ball in the air? The same gravity that pulls the ball down keeps our atmosphere in place. If Earth were smaller and had weaker gravity, the atmosphere would float away. Living things would not have air to breathe. Oceans and lakes would float away, too, so we wouldn't have water!

Earth's gravity keeps large bodies of water, such as the Gulf of Mexico, from floating away.

Do you have a favorite fruit or vegetable? Humans and animals depend on plants for food. Most plants get **nutrients** from the soil they grow in. Earth has soil that is good for growing food. Other planets have soil that is rocky or icy. Without soil, life as we know it could not exist.

Pumpkin patches can grow on Earth because of the planet's rich soil.

A Hard, Rocky Planet

Earth's surface makes it unique, too. It is a **terrestrial** planet with mountains, canyons, and volcanoes. Earth has land to walk on. But some planets are made of gas with no hard surface to stand on.

Fun Fact

There are two types of planets.

TERRESTRIAL PLANETS (mostly rock) are close to the sun. They are: Mercury, Venus, Earth, and Mars.

GAS GIANTS (mostly gas and liquid) are farther from the sun. They are: Jupiter, Saturn, Uranus, and Neptune.

Earth's tallest mountain range, the Himalayas, is in Asia.

We see our planet's surface all around us. It started forming 4 to 5 billion years ago. What land features do you see when you go outside? Do you live near mountains? A volcano? Flat plains? Or an ocean's shore? These are just some of the features of our amazing Earth!

You can even see Earth's
oceans and weather
from space!

GLOSSARY

asteroid (ASS-tuh-roid): An asteroid is a rock that orbits the sun. An asteroid hit Earth and broke off pieces that formed the moon.

astronauts (ASS-truh-nawtz): Astronauts are scientists who explore space. Astronauts have walked on Earth's moon.

atmosphere (AT-muhss-fihr): An atmosphere is the mixture of gases around a planet or a star. Earth's atmosphere is the air we breathe.

axis (AK-siss): An axis is an imaginary line that runs through the center of a planet or a moon. Earth rotates on its axis.

craters (KRAY-turz): Craters are large areas on the surface of a moon or a planet that dip down, like bowls. The moon has many craters.

dwarf planets (DWORF PLAN-itz): Dwarf planets are round bodies in space that orbit the sun, are not moons, and are not large enough to clear away their paths around the sun. Dwarf planets often have similar objects that orbit near them.

gas (GASS): A gas is a substance that moves around freely and can spread out. Earth's atmosphere is made of layers of gas.

gravity (GRAV-uh-tee): Gravity is a force that pulls objects toward each other. Gravity pulls Earth along its path in orbit and keeps us on Earth's surface.

nutrients (NOO-tree-uhntz): Nutrients are things that help people, plants, or animals stay healthy. Earth's soil has nutrients that help plants grow.

orbit (OR-bit): To orbit is to travel around another body in space, often in an oval path. Planets orbit the sun.

solar system (SOH-lur SISS-tum): Our solar system is made up of the sun, eight planets and their moons, and smaller bodies that orbit the sun. Earth is the third planet from the sun in our solar system.

terrestrial (tuh-RESS-tree-uhl): Terrestrial describes planets that have firm land, like Earth. Mercury, Venus, Earth, and Mars are the terrestrial planets in our solar system.

FURTHER INFORMATION

BOOKS

Goldsmith, Mike. *Solar System*. Boston: Kingfisher, 2004.

Trammel, Howard K. *The Solar System*. New York: Children's Press, 2010.

Wells, Robert E. *What's So Special About Planet Earth?* Morton Grove, IL: Albert Whitman & Company, 2009.

WEB SITES

Visit our Web site for links about Earth: **childsworld.com/links**

Note to Parents, Teachers, and Librarians: We routinely verify our Web links to make sure they are safe and active sites. So encourage your readers to check them out!

31

INDEX

ABOUT THE AUTHOR

L. L. Owens has been writing books for children since 1998. She writes both fiction and nonfiction and especially loves helping kids explore the world around them.